Scrap Paper

Jahnavi Fernandes

BookLeaf Publishing

India | USA | UK

Presentation by *BookLeaf Publishing*

Web: www.bookleafpub.com

E-mail: info@bookleafpub.com

ISBN: 9789358316339

First edition 2024

For Anji, Daddio, Mama, & even Jango

To Be Young

To be young is to have the entire world ahead of
you.
to hold the earth in the palm of your hand
To be blamed for crushing it
Before even stroking it
with our long, diffident fingers
poking at every dot
at every scar

To be young is to be scoffed at for immatureness
By the "mature" mess of those who were young
before us
Those who had the chance but lost it
Those who condemn us as the future but don't
confirm us as good
Those who created Kryptonite
But scolded us when we looked at it.
Those who forget Superman was Superman
because
He didn't listen to his elders

To be young is to be Batman and the Joker at
once.
It is to be full of life and never tired

To be young is to be insecure but confident all at
once
To be young is to be stupid but a genius when
colleges look around
To be young is to be waiting to grow up
To be young is to not want to be it.

This Chain

Am I Lightning
An illuminant signal in skies
To dramatize the rain
And pierce Father Zeus' enemies?

This chain,
The thumps of thunder are kitten cries.
Wicked warriors could wound my world
Yet its crystals would still shine like sun

It laces my neck
With a jewel to fall on my heart
To comfort like Aphrodite's necklace
To convince me that I am just as beautiful
To confirm me as Father's favorite.

Or perhaps
I am Hades
This chain draws meaning from other worlds
Holding ancestors who once held me
Gravitating to the solace of their arms once
more.

For Hestia has blessed me with a line of love
And until the stars connect to call me home

This chain of family αγάπη
Is perfect.

Slow Down

slowing down is a bike passing you
after telling everyone you had a car
and you watch it for a while knowing it is best to
let it pass
even though your soul fuels you to move
it commands you to keep going
for the car's sake
for the destination's sake
for the sake.

Pure destiny in dreams
for all your hope drove into the adventures of
your mind
but moving means crashing and burning once
more so instead
you sit with the fuel until it
exhausts out.

Fire

Oh! those flames which fury bright as sun
reviving the dreams of war men
oh, so frightened and frayed but
those nights of pure treachery
when Earth bears red arms
we can't forget
that Water
will still
win.

Air

bitter cold whips my hair as I
make my way through the long road ahead
the leaves marry birds as they float far

bright leaves blowing against itself
trusting the wind to take them
to the right place.

it floats far east and
swerves round the corner
into the distance

and never may I see
where it lands
but I know

In the end
it ended up someplace
good.

Earth

When I was younger my head used to
Spin like the planets round the sun
Bursting with thoughts until burnt
To the core and shriveled.

I wish I was her
Because back then
Her flaws were
Not real.

Now they just might be.

Water

The depths of sea seemed
Endless as I watched the sun
Reflect light off waves

Waiting Room

They say the fear of the pain is worse
Than the pain itself
but the fear seems to trickle down my toes as
blood rushes from it
turning them bright blue.

I want to believe
Fear will leave
but the fear shouldn't replace

regret dawning
and the gnawing
In my stomach
as it catches butterflies,
shimmying round as fast as my feet,
my blue, cold feet
which accent
a frostbitten mind
and flaming fear

As I wait.

Things We Think

The Earth was flat
Until Columbus didn't fall off it.
All those people who told him it was
And instead all he did was
Go too far west
And bumped into South America.

And then he brought gold back because
Gold is supposed to be rare or something like
that
But I think fool's gold's just as pretty
If you give it the right light.

Somebody also said sun days are supposed to be
beach days
But that person clearly never went to the Jersey
Shore on
A warm cloudy day and suddenly had a private
oasis
Because somebody said cloudy days are for
sobbing.

And the lemons that you get in the summer
Aren't really that sour
Yes, thinking they're sweet

Won't make the sour go away.
But it sure does help.

Like Pink

Like Pink
After Meg Kearny

I believe that pink is an attitude far more than it
is a color
I believe that smiley red lips beat clawed red
nails
And that strawberries are best lukewarm over
cold

I believe that warm orange sunrises are best
during gloomy snowstorms
The slow sun simmers and shimmers down an
icy cloud
Blazing and burning in its triumphant return
after the dark
I believe that bagels are best when the
orange-yellow crust shines like gold
I believe the orange-yellow bagels are only in
NJ

I believe in yellow sundresses lazily fluttering in
summer breeze,
Spinning and dancing and falling ever so quietly.

I believe in bright yellow taxi cars whizzing by
in Times Square
Always going somewhere, doing something
But the subway beats taxis anyday
I believe that dandelion weeds are the most
beautiful flower
I believe in the golden fries at the bottom of the
bag

I believe that 1954, being smart, and country
music are all green.
I don't believe in country music but I respect it
I believe that street smart is smarter than book
smart
But the smartest are those who struggle
I believe in spontaneous road trips by fields of
strawn out grass
I believe that trips don't solve problems
But they sure do help you forget
A nostalgia of the last road trip that's so jumbled
it's exciting
Or maybe it's just happiness

I believe that a sapphire sky day is always a
good day
But a good day doesn't always have to be a
sapphire sky day
I believe in the pearls at the bottom of the ocean

Because the rough tide world needs a smooth
treasure
I don't, and never will, believe in blue Christmas
I believe that Christmas season is better than
Christmas Day itself

I believe in lavender fields on windy days
Hair down, flying messily
As long as lip gloss is nowhere to be seen
I believe that Speak Now is the best Taylor Swift
album
And that Long Live is the best song on it
Even if you have to go through the whole album
to find it
I believe that grapes are a lot like people:
The bunch is sweet
Although some are just plain sour

But most of all, I believe in the rainbow
I believe in the childish magic of believing
I believe in the gold pot at the end of it
And all the colors hidden in between
Like pink.

To Tutors Who Charge $80 An Hour

The girl
She looked at me like an ant
From her tall pedestal that only she can see
"$80 per hour"
And then she smiles
As if I should be happy that she hasn't squashed
me yet

If you charge $80 an hour as a tutor
Can I just say
I hate you
I hope your life sinks as low as my math grade
I hope you bite into a chocolate chip cookie
And it ends up being oatmeal raisin
But most of all
I hope you struggle
I hope you try
And try
And fail
And do everything the right way
Only for life to go left
I hope you feel cold and bitter and numb.

But I do hope the winter melts

And that the bitter wind becomes a delicate
spring breeze
But when it does
Please keep an icicle in your pocket
So that you remember that somewhere
Winter is beginning
And when you meet a person shivering
I hope your cold heart thaws to gold
And you help them

Because being helpful
Is not profitable
It is not for the privileged
Nor is it exclusive for the pristine
Help is for the helpless
Be a nice human.

Starlight

Starlight, so bright
but never may it take a dime
and never may it take a pain
nor cure the black in my bones

moon sky, so full
enough to mock
my vanquished heart
as hearty flesh plunges
one by one
till a corpse remains

restless eyes,
stings my irises with
its luminescence
strikes a great grief upon
my spine which
trickles
to my phalanges
to numb them with
my hope

wish I may
wish I might
see thy end
dawn near

9-9:12 PM

Aloud and allbright
Blowing noises erupt with the wind of the book
Cackles and laughter under layers of blankets,
Dividing the world and the life for a little while
because
Every little love for books and every little love
For reading and writing, for daydreaming of
Green grass with blue skies with the perfect tint
of pink all was
Harvested in those bedtime stories.
In those little moments
Just between 9-9:12 was just so perfect as a
Kid, because the comfort and
Love were what made home.
Making memories that molded a
Nine-year-old into a teenager.
Opened the lock to a
Preciously powerful door just for me. And in
that
Quiet world of wonders there lay
Roads engraved in gold
Straight to a golden passion
To a golden life with an
Underlying frolic of

Vehemence for literature, because numbers are
for nice futures but
Words are for the wonderful,
Xenial ones
Yelling and crying and reciting and writing all
started with a
Zillion little stories from 9-9:12 PM.

A Letter to Mother Nature

I loved you
But I didn't want you
I loved your long hair and how it changed like
the wind
Painted a green and blue haven
My heaven

And my hell.

You dirtied my hands till it could do no more
Romanticized my brain till it could think no
more
Think of nothing more than this other green in
my pocket
That light, dark green
Green of glorious glowing growing greed
Angeled my eyes, deviled my heart.
It screams a treachered dare
And flaunts in the air
Because that green is rare
And you are

Everlasting.

And so

I kill you for the sake of sweet dreams
And till I learn that not all is as it seems
Until your hair doesn't change like the wind
And your greens look as blue as my heart
Maybe then

Changing Colors

When I was little I loved the color pink
I thought it resembled unicorns and princesses
All dancing in delight and dreaming of when
Prince Charming would come to save them.

When I was a little older my favorite color was
blue
My passions were about as big as the mini
satchel I carried
And though nothing was ever in that satchel it
still
Felt like being mysterious and being different
was better than
Being happy

And when my black boots cranked on floors
With vintage jeans wider than my joys
I watched other girls walk down the halls with
pink headbands
And new watches

So I could ridicule at their desire to be generic
Because it was better to be unique than it was
to be happy

And somewhere along those years my favorite
color became purple
With pink as a close second and
I stopped caring
I stopped hoping the person behind me thought I
was unique
My cares shifted to hoping I thought I was
happy.
I started hanging out with those girls with pink
headbands
Until I got one for my own

And could walk along with them.

A Dress Ode

Home is where your heart is
But my heart belongs to you.
A confining, confiding corset
With a massive comfort
And massive presence
twirling
Your soft silk skirt swash
Like a swan's blanket over crow legs
spinning.
A shield preserving me from the pretentious
pristine people on the outside
For a mysterious marvel you are
Take up the room, take up all your space
In the most delicate way possible.

Our Fate & Our Fruit

We are the bearings of some of the strongest
people on earth
Generations of war and bloodshed
But we are here
Lasting now
We are the survivors

We are the survivors of the cries for help and
runs for hope
The swords of hate touched many

But not us

Our smiles curved down in inferiority should
laugh in superiority
Because the rarity of their victory
Should be proof of our luck

For we are the fruit of resistance
The rise from the ashes
The ones who said no
To the plagues and poison
The ones who said no
To fate
The ones who said no

We can do this

We protest the failures
Because in the face of mankind's greatest
tortures
We laughed and held on to the hands of our
mothers
Our mothers who raised mothers to believe they
are great
Our mothers who raised mothers who raised us
to believe
We are great.

A Little Book

I believe in the book of which I poured my heart
into
And in each printed word was a girl staring at it
Fidgeting and fixing each until perfect
In the eyes of its mother
Yet they still seem dull.

I believe in time
Most of these were written in the depths of night
After a day of ache I still held the pen
And wrote until all mended itself.

I believe these words were some of the best I
could have done.
In all its wonder and the eyes of its mother
it is not the best of the world
But I am proud.